The Bridge Under Construction

A Book of Poetry by Scott Caputo

BLUE LIGHT PRESS ◆ 1ST WORLD PUBLISHING

1ST WORLD
PUBLISHING

SAN FRANCISCO ◆ FAIRFIELD ◆ DELHI

Winner of The 2019 Blue Light Book Award
The Bridge Under Construction

BLUE LIGHT PRESS
www.bluelightpress.com
bluelightpress@aol.com

1ST WORLD PUBLISHING
PO Box 2211
Fairfield, Iowa 52556
www.1stworldpublishing.com

BOOK & COVER DESIGN
Melanie Gendron
melaniegendron999@gmail.com

COVER ART
Grace Cossington Smith
The Bridge in-curve (1930)
National Gallery of Victoria, Melbourne
Presented by the National Gallery Society of Victoria, 1967
© Estate of Grace Cossington Smith

AUTHOR PHOTO
Dennis Hayes

FIRST EDITION

Library of Congress Control Number: 2019951053

ISBN: 9781421836416

The Bridge Under Construction

Poems in this collection have appeared (some in earlier versions), or will soon appear in the following journals and periodicals:

Conches: "Russian River Retreat", "Mission Walk",
    "Panamá Dream", "Hike of a Thousand Steps",
    "Spiritual Ends", "Riegersburg Castle"
Credyn, 1ˢᵗ place online contest: "Stopped"
Haight Ashbury Literary Journal: "Where the Pumpkins Go",
    "Cello Suite"
Haiku Journal: "Hike to Almeria Falls"
Poetalk: "The Bar", "Menswear"
River of Earth and Sky: Poems for the 21st Century (Blue Light Press):
    "Memories of a Preemie"
"Memories of a Preemie" nominated for The Pushcart Prize

Acknowledgments

I thank my beautiful wife, Melissa, for her love and support.
I thank my parents, Steve and Sharon Caputo, for their love and
    encouragement;
I also greatly appreciate
    Diane Frank, for being such a great poetry teacher and for
    pushing me hard to make this the best book possible;
    Kirston Koths and all the members of the "Poets Across the
    Bay" writer's group, whose feedback I have valued so much;
    my manuscript readers, Melissa Caputo, Steve and Sharon
    Caputo, Patrice Haan, Kirston Koths, Fred Ulrich, and
    Priscilla Wathington, who gave me such helpful feedback.

Contents

III.

I.

When I was beginning to read I imagined
that bridges had something to do with birds...
the longest bridges have opened their slender wings

—W. S. Merwin

The Bridge Under Construction

after a painting by Grace Cossington Smith

Through the window, I watch the steel arch trusses,
rising as wings,
pumping to reach the tip of sky,
the flight awakening inside me.

The granite concrete pylons sink
into the bedrock of the bay,
waters that submerge me
when I close my eyes at night,
suffocation
then release,
the joyful floating under starlight,
every gesture and word, kind or unkind.
Painful moments cling
to the inside of my rib cage,
fueled by unseen light
I can never touch.

From the pylons, the iron span
cantilevers from one shore,
reaching as a hand to another hand.

Every day, there is the longing to reach across:
I have been here for so long.
Am I ready to go over there?

As the weeks of anticipation pass,
I watch my wife in the mirror.
She carries the entire bridge inside her,
all of the steel pins, human bones, small and fine,

fastening and wrestling with gravity.
As each rivet finds its place,
the bridge discovers its strength.

At night, the cranes with their swaying hooks
rest on the outstretched points of the arch.
Moonlight silhouettes them;
sleep seizes every joint.
Days pass before the cranes move again,
before growing cannot contain itself anymore.
You have found me. I am coming.

The day the hands embrace,
the day I hold my son, chest to chest,
the bridge is no longer an idea,
but my new way home.

Stopped

Evening commute — wrinkled newspapers on the train floor.
Tip tap of my laptop interrupted
by braking moans, then the unfamiliar, terrible
crackling underneath our seats
like a vacuum sucking up needles— was it a car, was it —?
The train stops midway to nowhere.

Then the conductor says:
There was a trespasser on the tracks.
A trespasser. I knew what that meant.
There were no fences guarding these tracks.
Only small signs with red hands and a phone number.

The newspaper had just reported tales of train engineers
facing those desperate few, futilely blaring the horn,
maxing out the brakes
as a fragile stick of life wavers in front of the engine.
Engineer to suicide. Human to human.
Have you felt this pain before? Never like this.
Those last glimpses before the train hits.
Cold force of fuel and steel.

Today, the conductor says it was a young woman.
I wonder why?
Poisoned by grief? Unbalanced by love? Homeless in life?
Some passengers call up friends, morbidly replay the scene:
The train creamed her. There's nothing left.
Others bemoan the long hours of inconvenience:
Why did it have to happen today? I need to be somewhere else.
I think: *someone lost her baby today.*
A child 30 years ago kept grabbing the bloody rope
until it pulled her here,
pulling her down below the earth
and flashing lights.

Deepwood

In the shadow of century old oak,
I witnessed my first wedding —
my uncle, bearded, smiling
his new wife in Easter Lily white,
my cousin, not much older than me,
standing rigid in a mini-tuxedo,
the sticky summer air heavy with lilacs.

I was young and fidgety,
wanted to explore the trails
disappearing into the gardens.

The draped tables by beds of irises
floated around me.
Marriage. Second marriage.
The first ripples in the pond of my mind.
I didn't hear the dark whispers that day,
polite voices edged with regret,
my mom grieving my uncle's first marriage.

After hours of meandering
in small pastures around our parents,
my cousins and I were released!
We raced through the maze of hedges,
swung open the lattice gates,
tumbled into gazebos,
found hidden box gardens,
slick lawns in deep shadows.

We went deeper,
where the manicured shrubs opened
to wild pine and maple trees,
a forest trail leading somewhere unknown,
a creek gushing nearby.
We could hear it, each one of us,
that spring that would overflow our lives.
Someday it would be our turn.
But we were young, wanted only to spy
through the brush to the silver streak of the creek.
We pushed through the leaves, onto the edge
of the rush, reached out our hands
deep into the cold torrent.

II.

Nothing but me is moving
on these bridges
as I always knew it would be

—W. S. Merwin

Where the Road Leads

I've never been across this bridge before.
I strain to peer out my car windows
as the bridge arches toward the sky.
My first glimpses of the Bay:
shimmering marshes, orange ponds.
My life is suddenly expanding in all directions at once.
My first real job starts tomorrow morning.

I take the first exit off the highway,
follow the dusty state park road
around to the edge of the Bay.
I watch herons skimming the water,
the stream of cars across the bridge.

An orange tile staircase
spins upward to the roof of my office.
My desktop view cuts across tops of trees,
lakes of leaves hovering in liquid air.

My first weekend after work, I notice
the brown, rippled foothills,
and decide I must drive until I reach them.
I think about my first programming assignments —
highways of variables intersecting and climbing,
networks of nodes expanding and collapsing,
arrows pointing upward and outward.

I turn into a neighborhood
under the shadow of the hills,
wind through quiet streets, avoiding cul-de-sacs,
until I'm stopped by a three-car garage,
the backyard melting into the hillside.

I watch the ridgeline for a while,
the flicker of color, the wavering cloud light,
hoping for movement,
for something to emerge.
The sun hides itself, sending me home.

I fall asleep, dream of the night
before my interview two months ago,
when I had ventured from my hotel
through the dark orange underpass
and emerged into the glittering white nightscape
of cafes and outdoor seating,
the air thick with music.
I walked down every street and side street,
planting every scene of laughter and dining lovers
deep inside me,
seeds of future happiness,
waiting for the day
when the first sprouts would push through.

Homeless Guide

Crossing the empty lines in the record store lot,
a black man with graying hair approaches me.
He holds a bottle of cleaner and old newspapers.
I hold a bag of CDs.
Both of us shiver from the autumn chill.
As he washes my windshield, he tells me
he has been *clean* now for six months.
He's back home again with his two young boys.
I nod, watch him spray my windows,
then rub them away with wads of Toys R Us ads.
Any money you could spare would help buy my boys some new shoes.
I hand him a few warm dollars.

Before he leaves, I decide to tell him my story.
I still have moving boxes stacked in my living room.
I'm scared of my boss in my first job out of college.
I miss the rain in the fall, that sweet tapping on the roof.
Outside of routes to work or church or the grocery store,
I have yet to risk losing sight of my apartment.

He tells me, there is one place I should go.
Hidden Villa, he says. *You should definitely go there.*
What is it? I ask.
He shakes his head. *It's so beautiful this time of year.*
I could only get adjectives out of him:
Golden. Secluded. Peaceful.
He gives me directions:
Take your next left. The air is so sweet. Then go right. Gorgeous leaves.

His excitement inspires me
to find this magical place.

I drive through laurel-lined back roads,
discover the vast mountain forests
just beyond the suburban yards.
I arrive at a pair of tire tracks in the dirt
leading to an old farmhouse
and a community garden sheltered by maple trees.
I open the wide gate,
hear a swirl of wind chimes.
I step through drooping corn stalks,
dried-up oregano, and piles of shriveled squash.
I wonder why he loves this place so much.
It seems a hundred miles
from the record store parking lot.
I sit a while on the bench, breathing in rosemary and hay,
wondering how long before I find my hidden home.

Trail Repair at Purisima Creek

Twelve volunteers stand in the hot morning sun,
many of us still wearing our faded collegiate letters.

Our leader pulls into the trailhead lot, a pickup full of tools.
He directs his recruits to carry
12 x 1 foot planks, 3-foot metal stakes,
a post driver, shovels and sledgehammers.

Our work site is deep in the woods,
a section of trail where the hillside
has overrun the path.
The journey will be several miles in on foot.

I pick up one side of a plank with another guy.
Who will ask for rest first?

We start through dusty scrub,
descend into knots of fir and madrone.
Down bends and switchbacks
I balance my load, wishing I had gloves
against the grain, my muscles pinched
as if by hot prongs.

The weight of wood crushes my sternum
down fern covered slopes
winding over rocky juts and old stumps
following a trail someone else had made.

I finally rest, as do others.

But our leader gets us moving again
into the darker shade of redwood,

the faint rush of the creek ahead,
a roar waking itself up.

My biceps are burning rocks
by the time we reach the site.
I am already spent
but the real work still needs to be done.
We put down our loads,
slap our arms
before attempting to beat
the metal stakes into solid earth
that pushes back
with all its might.

We take turns
pounding stakes:
sledgehammer, post driver,
sledgehammer.

I swing with fire
only to budge the stake
a little.

I attack it,
grunt,
bellow —
still little.

Other men do so much more
seem so much stronger,
yet even they tire quickly.

We strike, strike,
drive, drive
the stakes,

determined to puncture the earth
but it yields only just enough.

Finally, we lift the long planks into place,
only a tremble of power
left in our arms,
heave and press the wood
against the restless slope,
sliding it behind the stakes.
I can barely move.

All of our work
measures only a few paces.

We hike up the grade
carrying only the tools.
I let others struggle
as I shuffle through shadows,
to my car, to my bed
to a nap that will consume
the rest of the day,
shocked at how lacking I was found
doing the work of men.

Moving After Dark

On those late nights I arrived home from work
just as the apartment sprinklers sprang up,
curious sputtering of liquid sparks
that exploded into a hissing mist.
I slid through the damp air,
my eyes dry as sand
from staring at a monitor twelve hours,
my whiteboard of competing tasks smudged together,
my startup deadlines threatening failure.

I was a castaway in my own life
avoiding my boss
who paced the halls, grinding his teeth.
I had no place to replenish myself,
stranded under fluorescent lights.

Yet, during this time of emergency meetings
and empty break rooms,
I decided to find a new home.

For years, I never had time to move,
complacent before the TV flicker.
But from long hours of building a new company,
lines of code laid as bricks,
the desire for the unexplored possessed me.

I had to find a new neighborhood
the one I always dreamed of living in
where I could walk to croissants and tea in the morning
and thin-crust pizza at night,
where I could walk past family homes with lawns,
not streets withdrawn into apartments.

Those first evenings after the move,
I stumbled into a living room full of boxes
and disassembled furniture,
with not even a lamp to turn on,
or a free chair to relax in.
I had to crawl between rows
with a flashlight
looking for the box with my bed sheets.
I wanted to plunge into a pillow,
but I needed to set up my nest.
My hands, sore from typing all day,
put away glasses and spices.

It was crazy to do this now,
but I had to test myself.
These nights of strain would come and go.
Could I endure?

Late one night, from my office window,
I saw a utility truck rumble in below,
a piercing spotlight switch on as a utility worker
descended a manhole
into the dark underground
to probe with only a small light.
The light finally turned off,
as I went home to the sprinklers,
wading through those streams of water
that were always gone by morning.

Where the Pumpkins Go

Down the empty rows of the pumpkin patch
I see the rejects, collapsed from inside.

Unbound from a bale of memory,
a fourth-grade field trip to a pumpkin farm.

The school bus amplifies our rising chatter.
Hay bale towers part to reveal a sea of orange.

Happiness can be weighed on an old scale.
Each pound promises more fun.

A glowing grimace on our Halloween porch.
How did I get so lucky?

Now, broken pumpkins litter my path.
They should never be given to any child, but they are.

Some of my classmates took home pumpkins
already rotted to the core.

They tried to carve them,
but some of my classmates are already dead.

Some are paralyzed. Some got caught
in the sugared rush of addiction.

Some simply disappeared,
no sign save a clipped vine.

I look for the pumpkin
passed over but still beautiful.

I bring it home to remove the guts,
watch the droopy insides burn.

Shinkansen

Chris calls it train surfing.
We stand in the center aisle
palms outstretched
feet pressed forward
ride the thrust
as the shinkansen
rips through rice fields at 80 mph,
every village a quick burst
of white static.

We are determined to fly at breakneck speed
through the unexperienced world
for late night jaunts to neon clubs and bamboo cups of nigori.
We are kings of the moment,
two six-foot giants crushing for a good time.

Chris raced out of our childhood town
for hot Japanese sake and steaming onsen.
By day, he teaches English to Japanese high schoolers.
By night, he chases local girls,
singing karaoke in tiny bars.

Still, after years of trying, he has not found
the girlfriend that will become his wife.
And neither have I.

Chris and I exit the train into the old alleys
of Kyoto, meander among jazz bands and shakuhachi flute,
see the painted maiko click clock on wooden feet,
finally find our ryokan, the old inn for travelers,
the room empty except for futons on tatami mats
and a pot of sencha leaves waiting to be brewed.

Representing Me

I don't want to hear from you, my congresswoman sneered.
I felt as if she had slapped my face.
She put her arms around the undocumented
teenagers in our delegation who spoke of their desire for college.
We crowded her in the spacious congressional office,
walled in by stories of her accomplishments.
All of us--white, brown, black, men, women,
had come across country
to ask her to support children's healthcare.

But I could hear the accusation underlying her voice:
Who the hell are you to talk to me?
I was too white, too male, too educated, too sheltered.
What did I know of pain or discrimination,
or of getting paid less for the same work?

Now, it's your turn to feel shame, her voice seemed to intimate,
the pulse-pounding shame of being yourself,
of finding your gender and the color of your skin lacking.
You have no worth here.
Go home. Go hide in your condo
in front of your computer
drinking in your privilege.

What did I know of life on the other side of the fence,
where opportunities are guarded by barbed wire,
where parents face their hungry children every day?

I was always regarded as smart even before I opened my mouth.
What if people had looked at me differently my whole life,
doubted my skills and motives,
thinking I was inferior before I proved them wrong?

I always had everything I needed.
What if I had no place to study,
no breakfast every morning,
no father who lived at home?

Our delegation leader noticed I was shaken up,
took me aside later:
She was wrong to talk to you that way.
We chose you to represent the community.

Our delegation ate meals together, laughed together.
I shared a hotel room with a Mexican man.
We were different in every way,
but we were here for the same reason,
to advocate for the asthmatic kid
with no inhaler,
the diabetic with no monitor.

What would be my contribution?
Sit in anger over my last encounter
and imagine a fiery rebuttal.
Or walk with my group again
to another congressman's office,
be ready when our leader points to me,
shout out: *Will you support us or not?*
watch as the congressman falters for words.

Spiritual Ends

Down the dim halls of the seminary, I followed my friend.
Jeremiah, in beige robes, beckoned me
into the backyard grotto, a patch of woods
whittled away by freeway easements,
a remnant of wilderness within Berkeley's bounds.

Light crisscrossed oak crowns,
but every path I chose led to a giant web
strung from unseen branch tips,
a sly mass waiting for me.
The Novice Master eyed me closely that day:
a new recruit?

So many times I had contemplated the cloth.
A life behind confessional screens.
A heart held inside a tabernacle.
The eye of the monstrance peering into every soul.
So much light, but I feared the empty room at night
alone with only a crucifix.

My friend embraced the order:
philosophy papers on Kant and Hume,
a mission trip to Chiapas, Mexico,
summers at the McKenzie River House.
Along the way, his fellow novices
dropped out or were asked to leave;
one left to fight terrorists in Afghanistan.

Near the end, he would have to pass a final vote.
Would the order take him? How could they not?
My friend's spiritual charge had only grown.
No longer just my old college dorm mate

who liked to debate metaphysics,
but a man destined to be a Father.

The seminary elders, those who sat by themselves,
saw Jeremiah differently:
not eager enough to wear his habit,
not obedient enough to his superiors,
not correct enough in his moral thinking.

Their vote surprised everyone and no one:
Not yet.

Within a year, Jeremiah had shed his robes
to teach high school English.
Within another year, he was married to a woman
who had consoled him through his grief,
a fellow traveler on an intersecting road.

Then came children and fatherhood of another kind;
no priories or prayer five times a day,
but a different devotion,
waking in the middle of the night at regular intervals,
feeding a little soul,
lulling, lulling the self asleep.

Collins Street

after a painting by John Brack

Must get home, closed in by drenched office shirts,
frayed suit sleeves, stained eyeballs, bobbing,
dangling, focused linear exhalations, puffing,
must hurry past tenements, empty gray windows,
power lines extend far above, twisting,
slicing through tree trunks, cutting clouds into tatters,
killing, mincing curse words.
Someone farts, someone shoves, someone pushes someone down
stairs to the subway, stares of bearded shadows,
sidewalk slants, pits open, doors to subterranean
pools bubbling, pant legs pumping ahead, must get
away from copier malfunctions, hang-mouth managers
clawing at cubicle mice, streams of mutilated memos,
relentless pounding of keys, carpal tunneling,
skeleton-faced meetings, smoking coffee pots,
lost hours in the bathroom, toilet troubles,
the clock's tricks, the shredded calendar, one small window.
Must hurry home to river of gin-soaked, vodka-varnished,
olives floating on carpet spills, littered bottles,
blinking screen of legs spreading, mouths opening,
the flinging of dishes against the wall,
the midnight smoke, past midnight smoke, the smoking smoke,
sink full of salted fries, melted ice cream,
into the bedroom, the gun in the nightstand,
desperate search for one perfect thing,
finally, the release in the dark.

Menswear

after a painting by John Brack

Men come to me every day to alter their identity,
but I stay the same — only older.
Rows of orange mannequins, better dressed than me,
quiet in blazer, shirt and tie, no feet, only torso,
sometimes, not even a head.
I measure, I advise, my authority pinned on.

The 3-way mirror reveals everything:
notes from a mistress, receipts from unspoken encounters.
Some men imagine themselves important, smart, successful.
To cover our nakedness, we drape ourselves in silk and wool.
How do you measure a man? By height? By waist?
By power? By possessions? By anything?
Is the universal tape measure all zeroes? An infinite line
leading from the chest outward?

I see the same suits on corpses, their eyes closed,
their hands closed over pin stripes, three buttons.
The body sleeps in suits. We go before God in our last suit.
But I stay here. I hang fallen ties. I fold discarded shirts.
I keep everything neat until the lights go out.

The Bar

after a painting by John Brack

I am surrounded by men who don't see me.
They drink and smoke their lies together
in dark circles in the mirror.
I am fading yellow,
an old candle down to the stub.

I remember getting married,
wearing white satin.
That was a happy day.
That was before the war
bled through my life.

Another drink. Another round.
Every night I wait for the last round.
Alcohol and tears are stored
in bottles below the bar.
Our religion is the empty glass.

Did I know my husband?
Would he have grown cold to me too?
Sometimes, I see him
hovering among the dried-out faces.
The vase of gold poppies
illuminates my path to the door.

Reply All

Subject: How's it going?

Reply: Two roads in a forest diverged
and I clear-cut everything so I wouldn't have to choose.
And that has made all the difference.

Reply: So much depends on a red wheelbarrow
left in the driveway
being run over
by the white pick-up

Reply: The Lover. The Wise Man. The Heretic.
The Baker. The Candlestick Maker. The Butler.
The Colonel. The Detective. The Double Agent.
How did all of these strange people get in my poem?

Reply: 13 ways of looking at my sucky life. 1. My life sucks.
2. Everything sucks. 3. Suck my life. 4. Suck suck.
5. Life is sucky. 6. Sucky ducky. 7. Suckyville USA.
8. 24 hour Suck-a-thon. 9. Suck-a-saurus.
10. Suck-a-million. 11. Suck-a-palooza. 12. Life.
13. Sucks.

Reply: Fluorescent rods burn my inner eye.
Into the windowed room of consciousness.
At the top eave of the house.
Perched above a river of syllables.
From the first hour of my birth.

Reply: This is my poem. I am writing a poem.
I am writing my poem right now.
This poem may refer to other poems.

This poem may contain similes and metaphors.
This poem may be an extended allegory.
I should start wrapping up my poem.
This is the final line, the one you'll remember most.

texting while dying

pick me up some drive thru intimates
talk to you tomorrow face to effaced time
meet me in front of the ego building
running late caught in sex traffic
lol at your last messes
can't talk now with the departed head
need to meet for a drowning drink
left your shirt skin at my place
found your earring tone on my sink
hate commuting in my sentient car
need to find a better jawbreaker
looking to jump to a new sexual position
someplace with a view of the after death
want my own office teeth and hot cup of coughing
this joke is killing me

My Uncle's Church

My uncle's voice, steady and reverent,
mixes prayers and incense under wooden eaves,
rain strumming the church roof in November.

Through winter creek waters, his voice bears
across the barren fields of parishioners,
waiting for the last frost.

Many weekdays, he said Mass only to himself
at his coastal home,
a few candles and a coffee table as an altar,
then long hours of solitude.

The first time I made a confession,
my uncle listened
sitting across from me in full vestments,
nodding as my young voice cracked.
I was only a child, worried about my mom's scuffed-up floor.
I didn't know what sin was. None of us do,
until it moves into our heart and we let it stay.

How many confessions has my uncle heard?
How many tearful stories told in shadow,
a wooden screen protecting only their identity,
everything else laid bare?

As a child, I took so many things as given.
My uncle would always be there to say Mass.
Even if I was gone for many years,
I could come back to his small church
surrounded by open fields and farmhouses,

see him raise the bread and the wine,
share his homily,
before he finally took his seat:

I saw a tree once while I was out for a walk.
It looked green and healthy from afar,
but when I got closer, I could see the heart
was brown and dead.
I cleared away the withered branches
though there were many of them.
How many times are we the tree?

Panic in the Melbourne Jail

The foot-thick metal door swings closed.
People around me seem amused.
The girl next to me texts: *I'm in jail!*
But I feel a prisoner's chain drop into my stomach,
coil, clink link after link,
press against my ribs, my lungs,
pull me against the bench, down into the floor.
My skin blazes with flashes of heat.
My eyes blink rapidly.
How long before they open the door again?
Five minutes? Ten? Fifteen?
The man next to me asks, *are you all right?*
I peel off layer after layer of clothing.
I can't stop sweating.
He senses my distress, presses the inner panic button.
Someone is supposed to come and open the door.
No one comes. Then the lights go out.

I am back at my parent's house,
home alone, sweeping the garage—
all doors locked shut,
except the side door, open to the summer air.
Garage door nearest me
jerks up with alarming power,
but holds its ground.
The next garage door spasms in the same way.
Someone is coming.
They will find the open side door.
I need to hide. I need to escape.
All I can do is stand and grasp the broom harder.
A man barrels into the garage,
growls, *IS THERE ANYONE ELSE HERE?*

He's a police officer. My nervous hands worry him.
He draws his gun, tells me to *FREEZE! GET DOWN!*
Another cop emerges behind him,
bigger than the first, draws his gun too—
I stare at their guns. I imagine the heat of their bullets.
I hear them yelling at me.
One of them pushes me to the ground,
rolls me onto my stomach,
sticks his knees into my back, searches me.
The other keeps shouting,
WHAT ARE YOU DOING HERE?
ARE YOU HERE BY YOURSELF?

My words dribble out of my mouth like drool,
I live here. This is my house.
They hoist me up, have me lead them inside,
as I show them my ID, my family pictures.
They start to relax, laugh a little,
say I should introduce myself to my neighbors better,
leave me at the door, say: *Try to have a good day.*
I spend the rest of the day at home,
in my bedroom, in the family room,
wander room to room,
press against the warm glass of the windows.

Light rolls into our cell as the door groans open.
The warden reaches her hand out to us.
The girl next to me giggles, saunters out.
I pull myself up into the light as far as I can go.

Hike of a Thousand Steps

Water plunges down the orange crags
toward tops of pines
splashes through needles,
dissipates into brush.

Paul and I hike down the Giant Stairway,
cliff-hewn steps mixed with metal stairs,
hemmed in by the Blue Mountains of Australia,
every stride closer to cooler drafts.

I'm already tired
but how can I complain
when my friend does everything I do
with a baby on his back?
Little fingers
slap his sweaty hair.

Ten years ago in California,
Paul and I ran inside a closing gate
toward a monastery
we spied from the freeway,
a sprawling snake-line
with s-curved roofs.

No one stopped us
as we wandered
through wind-chimed gardens,
benches on the valley edge,
the last place missionaries saw
before they jumped to China
with only a book in their hand.
A passing monk took our photo.
Two friends against the ridge.

Now Paul is a world away in Australia.
As we march down each step,
the path turns. My friend tells me
how he holds his son
for hours every night.
But he's grown so fast,
already too big to nap on Paul's chest.

What have I done
with my empty apartment?
I have fallen
into the spaces between days.

The forest towers over me
as looming chimneys blacken the skies.
I can't stay in the shadows.
I must get ready to leap.

Journey's End: Phillip Island

The last hours of sunlight drain
behind dense storm clouds,
the first drops hitting our car, racing
to the Southern tip of Australia
toward shores of ice, glacial fingers.

Inside the car, my friends and I are warm.
Across the vast ocean, a light burns
in a San Francisco window
somewhere inside a wispy fog bank.

My girlfriend's disembodied voice
I heard yesterday
from computer speakers:
How are you? I miss you.

The rain slaps our cheeks
as we run inside the nature center,
walk through staged exhibits,
then race outside through pelting water
to roped-off sidelines in the sand dunes.

Crowds of tourists from every land
huddle in ponchos, wide-brim hats.
Germans discuss *die Pinguine,*
Japanese point at *Pengin.*

We are here to see Little Penguins
who, having spent hours fishing in darkening seas,
finally emerge together in waves
flippers on sand
click, chirp, chatter, march down lanes
surrounded by gawkers in slickers.

As penguins hop to their burrows,
they poke out again, calling
pleading for the swimmers still to return:
come home, come home.

The penguin parade thins out, as do the people.
Rain picks us off one by one,

I stay,
watch as one more
then one more wanderer
shuffles out of the ocean:
find me, find me.

III.

on the breathless night on the bridge with one end I remember you

—W. S. Merwin

Cello Suite

Submerged in the icy air of her bedroom,
the heat still broken in the worst days of winter,
my girlfriend and I hold each other for warmth,
entranced by Casals playing Bach,
an intimate concert only for us:
spray of starlight, candles awake,
whispers, hands full of satin,
spinning, fragrance of old roses,
coastal swells, dancing,
sunset then sunrise, open, open.

Everything is early.
Our shy hands are still learning
each other's bodies,
searching for warmth.

Deep in that pond of frozen air,
we swim upward into the resonance
of cello, stressed and delivered,
tensed and worshiped,
light of listening, stretching frame
of self and desire, words
dissolving into reverberation.

All night our hearts vibrate
a new music.

Panamá Dream

Anoche cuando dormía   Last night as I was sleeping
soñé ¡bendita ilusión!   I dreamt—marvelous error!
—Antonio Machado   —Robert Bly (translator)

The third hustler follows us, asking for pesos,
as we try to stroll the early evening streets of Mazatlán.
We escape onto a *pulmonia* riding by.

We swim through the gush of open air.
A wild mix of aromas—salty, sweet, spicy--
as the cart jabs hard down another side street.

Our first trip together as husband and wife,
both of us in a new place,
our fingers exploring the feel of our rings.

We hop off at Panamá. The dining room buzzes
with Spanish voices, *bueno, bueno, sí, sí.*
No one speaks English. No English menus.

We study the entrée list
with dictionary in hand. The murmur of foreign
conversation is both frightening and exhilarating,

like wading farther and deeper into the ocean.
Earlier that day, we had wandered through old town,
found a bookstore and an untranslated volume

of Machado's poetry, words I could not read,
but I could imagine the beehive,
the golden bees spinning honey inside.

que una colmena tenía
dentro de mi corazón;
blanca cera y dulce miel

Two plates bloom *carne asada* atop corn *sopés*
with a trio of red, green and yellow salsas.
Everything is drenched, flavorful beyond

any Mexican food from back home —
where our living room is full of boxes,
the merging of mine and hers into ours.

No one tells you how it should go.
The dessert cart rolls by like a magical carriage,
stacked cakes, frosted, drenched in *tres leches.*

I choose the plum cake dotted with purple domes;
my wife grabs a piece of *flan de kaki,*
caramel flan topped with dark chocolate cake.

We share bites, eager to taste each other.
Can every night be like this?
Kisses sweet with sticky *cajeta.*

On the taxi ride back in the dark,
my wife presses into me
into an air of dreams

lamps turning on and off,
friends coming and going,
endless breakfasts and dinners,

our shared breaths and heart beats,
my wife's stomach full and bare,
inside, the bees building their white combs.

What Can Be Held

I have no claim on you.
—Robert Bly, *Loving a Woman in Two Worlds*

Outside our Mazatlán hotel window
storm clouds rumble. Lightning strikes over the beach
as we delve deep into each other in the humid air.
My wife wears a turquoise necklace
against her bare skin
illuminated with each lightning flash.
I bought her the necklace today
as we meandered through old town,
the plaza palm trees shading us from the heat.

By next morning, the night clouds have been wiped away,
and we wake early to grab a beach cabana.
A breakfast of chilaquiles and waffles
brought from our hotel buffet,
then we gobble up mangoes from a wandering seller.

Another vendor promises a parasailing adventure, cheap.
I convince my wife she should try it.
Hey, it's our honeymoon.
Tanned men buckle her into the safety harness
then signal to the motor boat.
The ropes squirm back and forth, and then spring taut,
suddenly lifting her up, up, up
until she is only a grain of a person
under the wings of the parachute.
Soon, I see only the parachute
far down the length of the beach.

I look around, alone, in this foreign place,
Mexican words in my ear, a hot wind of language.
For a moment, I feel the ache
of all those years before I met my wife.
Standing alone in crowds,
returning home to an empty house.
I thought I had left them behind.

The boat speeds back toward the beach,
her form comes into view, arms and legs, then face,
as she barrels full force onto the sand.
The tanned men catch her, hold her upright.
She bounds back into my arms as if she had never left,
I could see our hotel; it's peaceful up there.
Even as she speaks in my ear,
her swimsuit against mine,
I can feel that holding her
is like trying to hold the ocean,
restless and deep.

Unbreaking

The train rumbles into the station ahead of me.
I sprint over asphalt, jump over track line
then trip. My wrist slams down
on the steel rail, a crackle of fire.
Train doors snap closed.

A snuffbox fracture, says the doctor,
pretending to pinch tobacco for his pipe.
Box of wrist bones
finely packed like family china.
Somewhere inside, a bowl shattered.
He soaks bandages in water,
winds them around my wrist.
The gauze hardens with each pass,
a handshake of cement.

Why did I do this to myself?
How can I go to London now?
How will I write reports for work
or lift my suitcase into overhead bins?

My wife, Melissa, holds me in bed,
my good arm around her,
my other arm propped up,
an animal hibernating inside my cast —
when will it wake again?

Come with me, I beg her.
My boss agrees. I will need help.
She drags, hoists the suitcases, our honeymoon luggage.
The long flight over, her head on my shoulder,
my wrist on a small pillow,
the long night behind white shades.

Our first London afternoon, we sit in bright museum air.
A three-tier platter of crustless cucumber sandwiches,
scones with clotted cream, swirls of lemon curd,
our faces submerge in saucers of tea.

Every morning, I pack into morning trains,
swing my wrist through convention crowds
while my wife takes the Underground
to some new museum to sit before a painting.
At night, we reunite in a wood-paneled pub
to quaff dark stout, savor steak and ale pies,
sticky toffee pudding.
In the king bed of our hotel,
our bodies arrive at new destinations.

At the open-air stalls of Borough Market,
we find a block of Comté, unwrap the brown paper,
memories from Melissa's student days in Paris —
art history hidden on every street,
baguette and cheese on some new corner,
every afternoon a surprise.

Our last day, we slip inside a neighborhood chapel,
unassuming from the outside, between apartments;
ceiling to floor stained glass, a breath of color.
As we stand by the altar,
I offer her the fingers of my bad wrist,
my tips touching hers,
bones of our one body.

Mission Walk

From the golden hours
of spring heating into summer,
we seek shelter under the long lattice tunnel,
spotlight of sun at the far end,
purple wisteria falling in our faces,
a cool breath of moist perfume.

On either side of the covered walkway
velvet red and yellow roses burn in brilliance.
The side door to the mission open,
the voices of the choir practicing songs of heaven,
timbre of chants and legato,
ocarina of blue bird trills,
murals of angel faces.

Only a year ago,
we were surrounded by wedding white orchids,
tables full of friends raising glasses and drinking champagne.
Then the honeymoon, first dinner parties,
first vacations, a whole year of firsts.
Still we are only two.

As we walk down the lattice path,
the spring soil turns under our feet,
the fountains whisper another calling
from the source of the well:
keep my garden green.

Unknown to either of us,
already new life has been implanted,
growing in the dark,
long strands of cords reflecting us both.

Russian River Retreat

entrance through the leaves
mud steps down to the river
stones curve in water

sitting on the pier
submerged in deep currents
soundless ducks float by

trees hover mid air
canopy of root hairs touch
thousands of rivers

Hike to Almeria Falls

crunch of leaf bristles
trail through the eucalyptus
breath of morning air

cirrus loops the sun
spirals up the coastal bluffs
faraway waves crash

fans of Queen Anne's Lace
droop over the inner path
florets full of bees

ridgeline trail mirrors
the river miles to the cliff
ponds live inside clouds

mountain waters blast
plumes of mist dampen the beach
toes submerge in sand

Skyscraper Rainstorm

Suspended in a thick downpour on the 12th floor,
I stare out at pinnacles of stone stretching
beyond my vision,
staggering twists and curves of quartz and glass.
Inside, I see
a soul gliding
through watery air.
A chasm of silence separates us.

Between these peaks, blowing rain
freshens the air, dampens the granite ledges
in patterns of mysterious clouds.

The rain falls with fierce certainty. It must fall,
even here,
even where nothing green can grow,
save a few rooftop gardens
and bamboo enclaves far below.

The rain must fall, and I watch it —
droplets stronger than I ever imagined,
closing the eyelids of the skyscrapers
that have nowhere to take cover.
The rain has seen greater than these —
faraway peaks taller than our highest plans.
We can only wonder how big the rain must be
to cover everything we ever built.

Emergency Overnight

My wife, Melissa, is strapped to the table
when I enter the operating room,
her arms spread crossways.
A pale curtain cuts across her torso,
shrouds the surgeons and their instruments.
Melissa twists, looks at me.
I stroke her face, tell her stories of when we first met,
our sunset walk at the coastal cliffs,
as the doctors begin the suctioning.

All night and all morning, we had waited for this.
Nurses padded Melissa's bed rails for fear
of a sudden massive seizure.
Her blood pressure, high, kept spiking.
Tests revealed low platelets.
Even if they could deliver the baby,
my wife could bleed to death.
Her blood brimmed with enzymes,
symptoms her liver was shutting down.
Her kidneys would soon follow.

The baby had to come out now.
Except, we still had two months to go.
Steroids were given to mature the baby's lungs,
magnesium to prevent seizures.
Would it be enough?
The emergency caesarian would be done tomorrow,
with the long night ahead.

They gave me a fold-out hospital bed —
too narrow, too short, too hard
but I needed to be near Melissa,
who jolted in and out
of panicked sleep.

My wife of only one and a half years,
my still unborn baby boy.
I needed them both
to stay here with me.

Nurses came as phantoms
every half hour
to poke and disturb my wife.
Our anesthesiologist appeared,
her voice calm as a pine grove,
I wanted to meet you
before everything happens.
I want to let you know
I will be looking out for you.

The priest came early.
What did he see?
A young family hanging onto life.
I watched as he rubbed oil on Melissa's forehead,
prayed for mercy for my wife
and our baby.

His first cries,
muffled, liquid mews
like a tiny kitten
alone in the rain.
He is here.
Wrapped in plastic,
arms and legs slowly moving.
Melissa, full of breath, says:
Follow him wherever he goes.
I'll be OK.
I squeeze her hand,
hurry after the
blue procession of nurses
pushing our son into life.

Memories of a Preemie

First memories
are newborn hairs
trailing off
soft infant heads.

So I hoped for my son
who lived his first weeks
in a heated box
hooked to heart monitors
a feeding tube
threaded up his nose
down to his tiny
walnut-sized stomach
all day a slumber
under bright blue
bleaching yellow
from his fresh skin
eyes closed
to the world.

Evenings after work
I scrubbed my hands orange
before entering the NICU
a room punctuated
by heart and breath
monitors beeping
suddenly screaming
before settling again.
Nurses rowed between
shuttered pods
cheerful blankets
hiding the one inside.

I held my son to my bare chest
let him feel my body heat
before putting him back
inside his incubator
for night after night.

My wife and I
hoped his first weeks
of solitude
would barely smudge
the mirror of his mind.

But months later
well after he came home to us
well after he learned to smile
we brought him back
to be with his former
roommates and nurses
a party with balloons and cake.

I did not expect how strongly
my son would embrace
his daytime nurse.
He last saw her when he was only
a few weeks old.
He gripped her with everything
a six-month old could give.
Somewhere deep inside
he was being held again
outside his glass box
human touch
timeless and warm.

Death of a Small Prayer Group

Up to the second floor flat,
my infant climbed each carpeted step,
thin arms and legs go, go, go.
How those arms and legs
twitched in the incubator six months before,
his eyes opening, shutting,
rhythmic movement, like prayer.

We need to focus more on God.
The words from my friend, Ella,
flashed warning to my heart:
she's distracted by my son.
Eight of us sat in a white room encircled by couches.
My son rolled around below us, tossing rings,
tumbling over pillow barricades.
How could she target my son?

Couldn't you just find a babysitter?
Not easily.
Couldn't you just trade off coming?
We were in this group first.

Our first night in the group,
a short walk from gothic spires,
crimson veil of light across San Francisco,
up the carpeted stairs to an oasis of couches,
my girlfriend warm against me.
Other couples reclined against pillows.
We ate. We laughed. We prayed holding hands.

One night after group, on the way back to our cars,
I led my girlfriend inside the glowing alcove, the Grotto,
where we had often shared a farewell embrace

suspended in candlelight and roses.
I surprised her, bowed, asked her to marry me.

One by one, two by two, people left.
New people came in, including Ella.
We traded evening for afternoon.
We bent more with every change.
But it was still church away from church.

I consulted my uncle, the priest, about Ella.
Who is this woman?
Her string of broken engagements,
relationships vanishing like incense,
intensely present then gone.
My uncle was clear.
Nobody should feel threatened by a child.

A jagged line fell between our group.
Some agreed our boy was distracting.
Maybe we should vote.
I love children. It's not that at all.
I need this group, she pleaded.
The resolution stalled. A flood of emails.
Rain followed by more rain.
Don't you see, this isn't fair. I'm a good Catholic.

The vote never came. She stopped coming.
Our first afternoon without her, clouds muted the room.
We felt the absence, but my son kept playing,
oblivious to the fragile structures we had built.

Only a few months later, our host had to move away,
and with that our venue and group disappeared.
This is all that was needed,
a final push to close the door, turn the lock.

Keys on the Highway

We merge onto the highway already anticipating
the comforts of home.
Clattering on the roof, then silence.
My wife and I twist toward each other — her car keys!

We have dodged calamity before:
her keys harmlessly
caught in the ski rack.
Not this time.

With no pockets, no free hands
while wrestling kids into car seats,
my wife often put her keys on the roof for safe keeping —
a glass of water on the piano
waiting to get knocked over.

I pull over to the rough shoulder
strewn with remnants:
windshield glass, socks, a reflector, a glove.
How many things are lost along the way?

I get out, smile goodbye to my worried wife.
Inside I am rage--too many nights of kids fighting sleep,
too many chores that stack up all day.
I never knew the years of work my parents did while I slept.

I walk down the edge
of the highway, cars speeding by.
I scan the pavement and scrub
for any sign of the keys.

In the weeds, I spy the remains of the key ring,
broken spiral, two keys twisted like paper,
yet a couple of keys and a clicker are miraculously
untouched, having missed the force of dark rubber.

I should stop, but I see more debris on the road,
more good keys and a fob split open like a clam,
the transistors inside glittering in the sun.
Would it still work?

I kneel down, reach with my fingers —
the displacement of trucks rushing
just a foot from my head.
Drivers jeer at me, honk "Hey!"

I stop for a moment, consider the danger,
snatch one key then another,
rivers of lives pounding past,
my fingers brushing the surface.

Riegersburg Castle

Ich nicht verstehen.
Why is it closed today?
The sign says it should be open.

I walk past my car toward the road,
an illuminated tunnel
of leaf and shadow.

Up to the field edge,
shards of soil twist up,
broken open to hold the future.

Beyond the stone fortress,
a patchwork of hills,
part cultivated, part wild,

my wife and sons far away
tucked inside a small house,
a sandbox and garden in the back,
lawns brown from drought.

My wife has been in our castle alone,
looking out, seeing everything
but not finding me.

Where have I gone?
My office has shelves of boxes
crammed with every bit

of dust from every dream
I had before I met her.
I just need to finish this last one.

In one box, the intricate
draftings of an inventor
lines carrying words carrying thought.

Easy to spend hours
lost in a room full of papers.
Somewhere there must be a path out.

Always one paper is missing.
That was a good idea.
Where did it go?

The children pile in around me —
Don't touch that.
Their eyes dance and discover,
hands grab and poke.

My wife comes from behind with a hug.
Come to bed. It is late.
I hear her voice

across the farms.
Take a picture of the castle.
The boys will love it.

Heart Work

Two months ago in my workout sweats,
I was jumping over rungs of a ladder,
stomping in and over lines,
when my heart sprinted ahead of me,
a motor I couldn't slow down.

My trainer barked, *Don't fall asleep.*
I was on the floor against the wall.
Someone brought me a cold towel.
I needed to go to work.
A paramedic with a bag approached me.
Sir, can you hear me?
I was supposed to eat oysters
with my co-workers at lunch.
My shirt was off, a stethoscope jabbing me.
Sir, please let me know you understand.
Every shell split open
the insides exposed.

The nurse shaved off circles of chest hair,
fastened probe after probe,
then switched on the gray screen.
My heart, a strange animal,
curved muscles pulsed, valves pumped,
every beat startled the eye.
What did I expect to see?
My wife's face? My children playing?
It looked mechanical and unfeeling.
Still, it was me.

Keep walking, the doctor said,
as the treadmill raced, tilted.
Keep going. Would the next incline be too much?
I ran, wondered if my heart would betray me.
Nothing was found. A singular episode.

Now I am in Belgrade,
pacing around at midnight.
Spotlights illumine the green domes,
the gold pinnacles of St. Sava.
Built on the site where the Turks
incinerated the relics,
trying to burn away rebellion.
Instead people raised stone ventricles
layer by layer
across hundreds of years.
The church is nearly finished,
everything except the inside.

The night air is warm leading me
through the Kalemegdan fortress,
all of the portals open, stone walls lit from below,
all the way to the last ramparts overlooking the Danube.

I am in a strange city
but the inner language is what I need to understand.
The fluttering in my chest, first there, then there,
then somewhere a door opens:
You must love this body.
You have made a promise to this body.

Farm Stay

The brochure showed a girl throwing seed to chickens,
a young boy riding a horse, vineyard hills behind him.
Spend a week in a trailer on a real working farm.

My wife saw the perfect family vacation.
Our family needed good memories.
What will we smile at when all we have left is a bed?

In the middle of our first night, our oldest son woke up
barking, wheezing, the terrifying throat-closing sound of croup,
cries mixed with breathing panic.

I drove to the nearest pharmacy, twenty miles away
mile after mile under the silent stars, darkened hillsides,
fields folding into fields, roads with no other driver but me.

The next few days, my sons, the sick one and the well one,
watched TV in our confined space while a heavy downpour
shook and rattled the walls, the farm taking in its yearly water.

During breaks in the storm, I sloshed down the back road
winding past old posts and thick trees, dodged puddles,
squeezed between the chicken coop and pasture fence.

Past the chickens, I found the stand-alone kiosk,
a store with no clerk. Wooden doors opened to reveal a fridge:
eggs, goat milk, yogurt, even blueberry cheesecake.

Money dropped in a slot, an inner safety hidden away.
I returned with my groceries; my wife was busy making dinner —
rich chicken noodle soup, a hunk of bread from home,

Soft-cooked eggs, warm runny yolks.
Our sons quietly sipped the broth, feeling the warmth,
the rain starting up again outside the window.

The Flying Fortress

My toddler boys and I duck under bay doors
right into the belly of the Flying Fortress
past vertical racks able to carry 8000 pounds,
bomb upon bomb upon bomb.

We walk around the aircraft, see multiple machine guns —
nose cheeks, waist guns, bathtub gunner, tail fin turret.

I imagine being stuffed inside a bubble,
the thrust of takeoff, the deafening drum of engines,
loading magazines, gunpowder choking the air.
Then enemy planes streak by, flaming bullets,
tattering the armor inches away from my head.

I hope my boys never have to go to war.
Their sweet faces don't know what a machine gun is.
To them, the Flying Fortress is a spaceship,
all wings, the shiny metal of dreams.

Sitting at a table is a real WWII pilot,
still flying stories at 92.
One engine went out and we had to break formation,
we were determined.
We lit up the refineries in Ploesti,
they came back at us hard.
We were surrounded by fighters.
We shot down two of them
before escaping into the clouds.

A Distinguished Flying Cross,
how could he have known the world he would save?
A world of television and cell phones,

where two people could be in the same room
and not even look at each other.

My lack of service shames me.
The boys and I climb back into our car,
talk about how much fun the air museum was,
another day of clear skies.

Grandfather Louis's House

I remember running into my grandfather's house
across hardwood floors into his lap for a story.
The same house his father, Domenico,
built from whatever scraps he could find —
tuna fish cans for junction boxes,
newspapers for insulation.
The whole house slanted into the hillside;
a marble would roll away if dropped.

I remember the kitchen where my grandmother, Lola,
stood at the old stove stirring her all-day sauce.
From that hearth, so many children were fed —
my grandfather and his siblings,
then my father and his brothers and sisters,
all enjoying the taste of asparagus and egg sandwiches.

I recall running up and down stairs —
the remnants of a second kitchen
when great Uncle Gene had shared the floors,
the basement built over a cistern
that fed water to the whole house,
the chimney of candelabra mosaic
designed by Domenico himself.

I recall sprinting down the sloped yard
into orchards of apple, pear, and cherry,
into patches of blackcaps and raspberries,
into plots of rhubarb, tomatoes, and peppers.
A mini Italian estate in the Portland hills
that even had yard chickens when Louis was a boy.

What did it mean to my grandfather
to live 77 years in the same house?
Domenico had built three houses on the property.
One by one they fell out of the family
until Louis's house was the only one left
of his father's legacy
until it too was sold,
for a tract home in the suburbs.

I imagined the move would kill him.

But in truth, my grandmother
and grandfather created a fantasy
around their new house: pepper flowers,
azaleas, rhubarb stalks, and dahlias,
the family oregano from Italy, towering foxglove,
a backyard patio of tomatoes and roses,
an inner garden he brought with him.

My Grandfather Returns

Last night, I dreamed my grandfather, Mike, was alive again,
back after more than 25 years
as if the funeral had been a terrible mistake.
He had spent those lean years in a secret hospital
along the Oregon coast
where doctors had slowly healed his scarred lungs.

Growing up, I remembered him struggling for breath
while he watched boxing, *Oh Lord, Oh Lord!*
Years of treatment on the coast had finally erased
the heavy oxygen tank from his side.

He sat on my couch, joked around just as I remembered.
How did you get so tall? Where did that height come from?
He was still an old man, not able to take care of himself.
He needed me.
My parents and I discussed where he should live.
I really wanted to take him in
for whatever years he had left.

Why was he back in my mind again today?
I remembered my cousin sobbing,
He's dead. He's gone.
I was in my last year of covered play yards,
soon to move to middle school
when he breathed his last
in a nursing home all by himself.

Maybe he was visiting me.
He wanted to let me know he was still watching over me.
He wanted to see my house

and meet my wife and two young sons,
including the one named after him.
Michael, that's a good name. How'd you think of that?

My earliest memory of him:
my cousin and I playing with cars in my room,
Grandpa, sticking his head inside for a moment
to get us to look up and laugh,
before he steps away into the next room.

Picking Oranges with my Sons

Dada, Dada, my boys squeal as the younger one tries to lift the picker.
The tall pole dips, wobbles. Caged hook clangs on pavement.

I steady the picker again. This time it thrusts
past branches, white blossoms, next year's harvest

to a dirty orange trapped between twigs. Struggle and tug,
almost like fishing. Tree clenches the hook, wrestles

until an orange pops into the cage, a satisfying thunk.
We slip it down, back through the maze. *Got one!*

My sons climb barefoot into the tree, up high the glowing crown,
a ring of unobtainable oranges, always out of reach.

Even accidents are valuable, when the picker knocks
an orange to the ground, the thick peel cracked with juice.

I guess we'll have to eat it now. I pry it open, a pouch
of gems, an explosion of sweet spray.

My dusty hands wash in gushing nectar.
I hold out wedges of sunlight for the boys to take.

Each runs off with their prize, their mouths singing.
Orange after orange drops into our bag,

soon to be zested, wrapped and frozen
for racks of walnut muffins in winter.

Orange halves pressed and juiced, each glass thick
with some secret happiness.

About the Author

Originally from Salem, Oregon, **Scott Caputo** has had a life-long love affair with writing poetry and creating games. His first book of poetry, *Holy Trinity of Chiles*, was published by Blue Light Press in 2010. His work has appeared in *Red Rock Review*, *Ruah*, *Haight Ashbury Literary Journal*, and *Saranac Review*. He also has five published board games, including *Völuspá*, based on the Nordic epic poem of the same name. He currently resides in Newark, California, with his wife and two sons.

www.ingramcontent.com/pod-product-compliance
Lightning Source LLC
Chambersburg PA
CBHW032028090426
42741CB00006B/765